Biggest,
Highest,
Fastest

Ian Rohr

sundance™

Published by
Sundance Publishing
33 Boston Post Road West
Suite 440
Marlborough, MA 01752
800-343-8204
www.sundancepub.com

First published 2002 by
Blake Education, Locked Bag 2022, Glebe 2037, Australia
Exclusive United States Distribution: Sundance Publishing

Design by Cliff Watt in association with
Sundance Publishing

Biggest, Highest, Fastest
ISBN: 978-0-7608-6689-4

Photo Credits:
p. 7 photolibrary.com; p. 10 photolibrary.com; p. 13 (top) Australian Picture
Library/J Carnemolla; p. 13 (bottom) photolibrary.com; p. 17 photolibrary.com;
p. 19 photolibrary.com; p. 20 Australian Picture Library/Corbis; p. 26
photolibrary.com; p. 27 photolibrary.com; p. 29 photolibrary.com

Printed by Nordica International Ltd.
Manufactured in Guangzhou, China
March, 2012
Nordica Job#: CA21200315
Sundance/Newbridge PO#: 226899

Table
of Contents

Biggest

A blue whale is definitely big. But how can an insect make it into the BIG category?

Blue whales can grow up to 30 meters (100 ft.) long and weigh as much as 30 elephants. They are the biggest creatures on Earth. While the blue whale and the elephant are big in size, other animals are big in different ways! They may have big noses or big teeth; or maybe there is a huge number of them. The BIG category is full of unexpected creatures—of all sizes and shapes!

Worm World

You might not think of worms when you think of big things. But think again. There are some very long worms out there!

Earthworms are found in the ground, and the biggest ones live in South Africa. These South African worms usually grow to about 1.5 meters (4.9 ft.), but ones as long as 7 meters (22.9 ft.) have been found. That's a lot of worm!

Tapeworms are **parasites,** and some of them live inside people. The beef tapeworm is the biggest of these worms. It is usually about 11–12 meters (36–39 ft.), which is about the length of a bus. But some big beef tapeworms have measured 25 meters (82 ft.)—about the length of two buses!

THERE ARE MILLIONS of earthworms like this in the soil. They digest and recycle the remains of plants and animals.

hooks

suckers

THE BEEF TAPEWORM'S HEAD has a ring of hooks and four suckers. It uses the suckers to attach itself to a person's intestine.

Q: How can you tell which end of a worm is its head?

A: *Tickle it in the middle and see which end laughs.*

Big Worms

There are about 20,000 different species of worms. These are some of the biggest!

South African earthworm

Beef tapeworm

Big beef tapeworm

Ribbon worm

feet	0	10	20	30	40	50	60	70	80	90	100

meters	0		5		10		15		20		25		30

Super Squid

You're on a boat at sea. Suddenly, an enormous creature with two **tentacles** and eight long arms covered in suckers rises from the water. It's a giant squid! Sailors long ago thought that giant squid were "monsters" that would grab them and pull them under the sea.

These super-sized squid roam the depths of the world's oceans. Because they can live in seas up to 1,000 meters (3,280 ft.) deep, we don't know much about them.

THE EYES OF A GIANT SQUID are the largest in the animal kingdom. Each is as big as a human head!

Still no sign of any giant squid . . .

Sometimes dead giant squid, or parts of them, are washed ashore. Scientists study these parts. They think that some giant squid could be up to 18 meters (59 ft.) long and weigh up to 900 kilograms (nearly 1 ton)! **Submersibles** that can travel into very deep waters may soon allow scientists to study living giant squid.

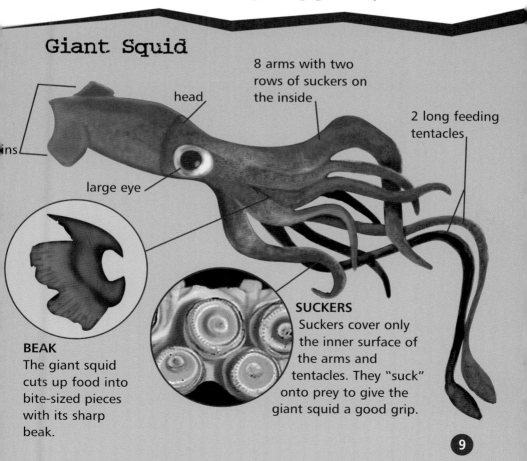

Giant Squid

head

8 arms with two rows of suckers on the inside

2 long feeding tentacles

large eye

ins

BEAK
The giant squid cuts up food into bite-sized pieces with its sharp beak.

SUCKERS
Suckers cover only the inner surface of the arms and tentacles. They "suck" onto prey to give the giant squid a good grip.

Big Parts

An animal can still fit into the big category even if its body isn't huge. Some animals have very large body parts compared to the rest of their bodies.

The fennec fox has 15-centimeter (6-in.) ears on a 40-centimeter (16-in.) body. Not surprisingly, this fox is a very good listener. It can hear termites in their nests and grains of sand moving when tiny beetles scurry past.

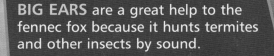

BIG EARS are a great help to the fennec fox because it hunts termites and other insects by sound.

THE LONG SPIRAL TUSK of a male narwhal grows from a tooth on its upper jaw.

Narwhals are relatives of whales and dolphins. The body of a male narwhal can be up to 4.6 meters (15 ft.) long, but then there's more! The males have a tusk that is about 2.5 meters (8 ft.) long. Male narwhals use their tusks to fight each other during the breeding season.

The Biggest of the Big

FANGS
Gaboon viper
50 mm (2 in.)

WINGSPAN
Wandering albatross
up to 3.6 m (12 ft.)

EYES
Giant squid
25 cm (10 in.) across

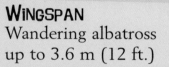

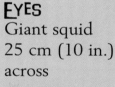

BRAIN
Sperm whale
7.8 kg (17 lb.)

EARS
African elephant
2 m long x 1.2 m wide (6.5 ft. x 4 ft.)

EGG
Ostrich
1.7 kg (4 lb.)

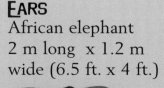

Number Crunching

What makes a small bug big? It all has to do with some very big numbers. Scientists have estimated that there could be 10 quintillion insects alive at any one time. That's 10,000,000,000,000,000,000 bugs, or 1.6 billion of them for every one of us. And about 8,000 new kinds are discovered each year.

Some insects, such as locusts, move in huge hungry groups called swarms. Swarms can contain millions of locusts. One huge locust swarm stretched from the Middle East to the Atlantic coast of northwest Africa. This was a distance of 4,000 kilometers (2,486 miles). To stay alive, every locust needs to eat its own body weight in food each day. A swarm of locusts strips trees bare and gobbles up crops. There are no crops left after a locust swarm has passed.

Locusts Lining Up!

Atlantic Ocean

Iran

Africa

Key

▭▭ Locust Swarm

A HUGE SWARM of locusts darkens the sky as it moves across the country in a feeding frenzy.

DESERT LOCUSTS like this one get water from the food they eat.

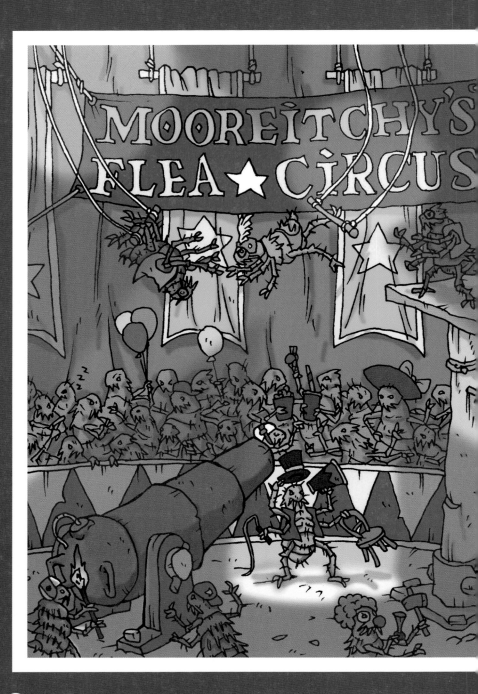

Highest

A flea? A giraffe? One stands very tall while the other is very small! How can they both be in the "highest" category?

The answer is that height can be reached in different ways. Giraffes make the record books because they are as tall as trees. Fleas are much smaller than giraffes, but for their size, they are the world's most amazing jumpers. The best human athletes are able to jump their own height, but fleas can jump 100 times higher than their own height!

Far-flung Fleas

A flea is only about the size of a pin head. But when it comes to jumping high, the flea is leaps and bounds ahead of us.

Fleas are parasites that live on other animals. They jump from animal to animal looking for food. Fleas don't have wings, but they do have rubbery pads in their back legs. These are squashed up tightly like springs until the flea wants to jump. Then with a trigger-click, the pads are released and the flea rockets 30 centimeters (12 in.) into the air. In proportion to its size, the force required for a flea to do its flip is immense. It is 20 times more than the force needed to launch a rocket into space! And fleas don't stop after just one jump! They can make these incredible jumps 600 times an hour.

Boing!

For its size, the flea is really the greatest animal athlete. For our size, we can't leap up with the same force as a flea!

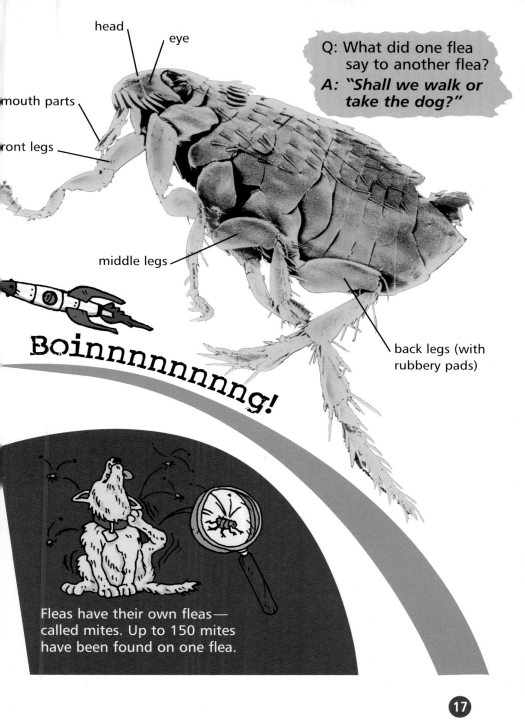

head

eye

mouth parts

front legs

middle legs

back legs (with rubbery pads)

Boinnnnnnnng!

Q: What did one flea say to another flea?

A: *"Shall we walk or take the dog?"*

Fleas have their own fleas—called mites. Up to 150 mites have been found on one flea.

Walking Tall

If you want a giraffe's view of the world, just look out a two-story window. At heights of up to 6 meters (19 ft.), the giraffe is the tallest animal on the planet. When a giraffe is born, it is about 1.8 meters (6 ft.) tall—the same height as a tall person. Giraffes are **mammals,** just like us. Like all mammals, they have exactly seven bones holding their necks up. But their neck bones are a little longer than ours!

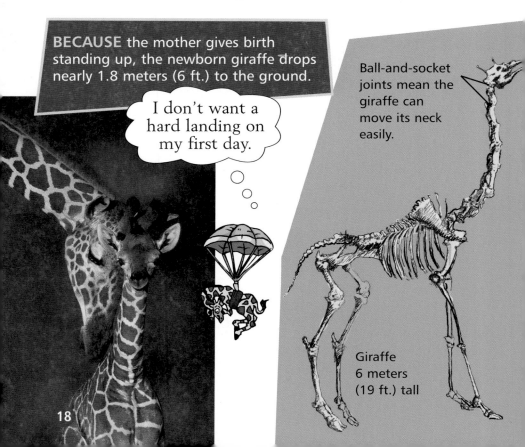

BECAUSE the mother gives birth standing up, the newborn giraffe drops nearly 1.8 meters (6 ft.) to the ground.

I don't want a hard landing on my first day.

Ball-and-socket joints mean the giraffe can move its neck easily.

Giraffe
6 meters
(19 ft.) tall

Human
1.8 meters
(6 ft.) tall

Giraffes can eat leaves from the tops of trees, but drinking is more difficult. They have to spread their forelegs out wide and bend way down to drink. Other giraffes keep a lookout for **predators** while the drinkers fill up as quickly as they can.

Flying High

Many birds fly high, but a Ruppell's vulture is the highest flying bird of them all. These **birds of prey** are not usually seen above 6,100 meters (20,000 ft.). But in 1973, a Ruppell's vulture crashed into the engine of a passenger jet that was flying at 11,278 meters (37,000 ft.). The jet landed safely with one engine. The Ruppell's vulture wasn't so lucky.

To reach such heights in the sky, a Ruppell's vulture has very strong wings and a very slow wingbeat. Like other vultures, it is a **scavenger**—it feeds off the flesh of dead animals. Once it spots food from the air, it begins to circle slowly overhead. Other vultures quickly arrive on the scene to join in the feast.

A RUPPELL'S VULTURE has spotted some food. It breaks its flight before landing on its prey.

Just how high do they go?

FLYING IN THE SKY	AT HEIGHTS OF UP TO
Ruppell's vulture	11,278 meters (37,000 ft.)
Whopper swan	8,845 meters (29,000 ft.)
Goose	8,540 meters (28,000 ft.)
Crane	8,540 meters (28,000 ft.)
Duck (migrating)	61 meters (200 ft.)

Fastest

The slash of a claw, the flick of a tongue, or an unexpected strike can mean sudden death.

There's a need for speed in the animal world. All creatures are part of a **food chain.** The trick is to catch what you like to eat, but not to get caught by what likes to eat you.

But fast isn't always about running. Fast can also be about the speed of a hummingbird's wings or about the flick of a chameleon's tongue.

All in a Flap

The hummingbird is one of the world's most frequent fliers. These tiny birds spend much of their lives fluttering from flower to flower. They are looking for **nectar** and **pollen** to eat.

To hover in the air when they feed from flowers, hummingbirds beat their wings an amazing 38–80 flaps per second. Some hummingbirds can flap 200 times per second when they are doing a power dive (usually to impress another hummingbird). This flapping takes a lot of energy, so hummingbirds need to eat every 10 to 15 minutes. And they don't waste time doing it. Their two-pronged tongues work quickly, licking 13 times a second.

Winging it!

Birds flap their wings at different speeds.

BIRD	WING FLAPS PER SECOND
Vulture	1
Gray heron	2
Herring gull	2.8
Starling	5.1
Pheasant	9
Mockingbird	14
Hummingbird	38–200

What was that?

THE MOVEMENTS of a helicopter and a hummingbird are very similar. Both can hover and fly up, down, forward, or backward.

Where's the nectar?

Q: Why do hummingbirds hum?

A: **Because they don't know the words.**

AT YOUR SIZE, you would have to eat about 130 loaves of bread a day to match the amount of daily food a hummingbird needs to eat.

Fast Food

Time for a snack . . .

The strike of a snake is quick enough to help the snake catch its prey. Some snakes, like the viper, lie hidden in the leaves—waiting. The combination of an unseen snake, a sudden strike, and fangs loaded with **venom** often means a quick death and dinner for one. Snakes might have to wait for their food, but they grab it fast and kill it swiftly.

THE VIPER SNAKE opens its mouth wide. Its fangs swing forward, and it is ready to attack.

Chameleons are lizards with a lot of talent. They can change color when they want to and move their eyeballs in different directions at the same time. And they are as quick as they are cool. The chameleon's sticky tongue, which can be more than twice its body length, shoots out like a whip at unsuspecting insects.

THE CHAMELEON has very good tongue muscles that allow the tongue to spring forward from the mouth and then pull back again.

Speedsters

Cheetahs are absolute speed machines. They have big hearts, lungs, and livers, which help them get great bursts of oxygen and energy. And they need it! In just a few strides, they can accelerate to nearly 100 kilometers per hour (62 mph) to outrun or catch prey.

Swift swimming stars is one way to describe members of the tuna and billfish family. The swordfish, sailfish, wahoo, marlin, and mackerel are better designed for speed at sea than sharks.

1 Coiled like a spring, a cheetah pushes off with one back leg and then the other.

2 It launches itself into the air, fully stretched out.

Long snout

Huge fin that sticks up like a sail but fits back into a groove when traveling at high speeds

Body shaped like a torpedo to power through the water

With their pointed snouts, long, slim bodies, and crescent-shaped tails, these fish are **streamlined** to slice through the water. The sailfish is the top speedster in this group of fast fish, reaching 97 kilometers per hour (60 mph).

3 Next, it touches down with one front leg and then the other.

4 As the body continues forward, the back legs touch the ground again. Then the cheetah pushes off once more.

RACING TO THE END!

FACT FILE

A man was found to have 143 tapeworms inside him. Their total length was 88 meters (289 ft.).

You'd expect the largest animal on Earth to have a very large appetite! Blue whales eat about 4 tonnes (4 tons) of krill each day!

Peregrine falcons are birds of prey, like vultures. They dive-bomb their victims at 300 kilometers per hour (186 mph). Look out below!

In parts of Africa, there are many swarms of tiny flies. People grab handfuls from the air and make them into cakes.

I must get my goggles fixed.

To escape from danger, a squid can swim very fast. It can jet-propel itself through the water by taking water into its body and then squirting it out through a breathing tube.